C000199659

HILLINGDON VILLAGE

KEN PEARCE

SUTTON PUBLISHING

Sutton Publishing Limited
Phoenix Mill · Thrupp · Stroud
Gloucestershire · GL5 2BU

First published 2007

Copyright © Ken Pearce, 2007

Title page photograph: Hillingdon Football
Club, 1898/9.

British Library Cataloguing in Publication Data
A catalogue record for this book is available from the
British Library.

ISBN 978-07509-4675-9

Typeset in 10.5/13.5 Photina.
Typesetting and origination by
Sutton Publishing Limited.
Printed and bound in England.

To my wife Pam
We first met in Hillingdon Village, and for over forty years
she has encouraged my obsession with local history.

CONTENTS

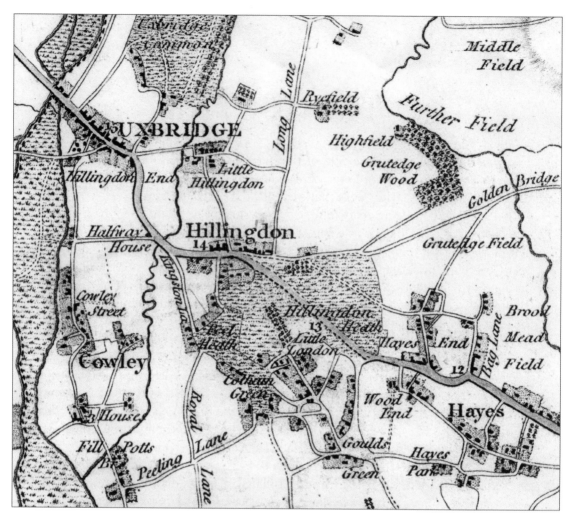

The first really detailed map of the area was drawn by a Frenchman named Jean Rocque, and a section of his 1754 'Topographical Map of Middlesex' is shown here. One is immediately struck by the large area of Hillingdon Heath to the south-east of the village, with even the main road to London passing through open grassland before reaching Hayes End. The fact that Long Lane, Royal Lane and Kingston Lane are marked helps us to get our bearings today. Ryefield and Highfield, probably farms, survive as the names of local primary schools. Peel Heath is now Pield Heath. Falling Lane is marked as Peeling Lane. The northern end of Vine Lane, where Hillingdon House and later Hillingdon Court stood, is marked as Little Hillingdon. Rocque might well be surprised to discover that Halfway House is now a fish-and-chip restaurant.

INTRODUCTION

The word 'village' in the title of this book may well be questioned by some readers. Can we still use that word to describe what was undoubtedly a village in days gone by? The fact is that we really have no alternative.

In 1964, when plans to reorganise local government in the Greater London area were being discussed, there was a fierce debate at Westminster over the name for the new Borough. The final decision was between Uxbridge and Hillingdon, and the result went to the latter. Thus it came about that on 1 April 1965 the London Borough of Hillingdon came into being, and to most people that is what the word 'Hillingdon' means today. All we can do to avoid confusion is to call old Hillingdon, the area at the geographical centre of the Borough, Hillingdon village.

My own connection with the village goes back to my arrival at Bishopshalt School as a pupil during the Second World War. It still seemed very rural, with Mr Bunce's cows walking up and down Royal Lane twice a day to be milked. After seven happy years there I left for a decade, and then returned as a teacher for thirty-two years. Since my retirement I have continued to keep in touch with the school, and am at present the honorary archivist. A great deal of my life has therefore been spent in Hillingdon village, and I have had the opportunity to observe and study it at close hand.

My family's connection with the village goes back even further. One branch of my mother's family, the Buttrums, arrived in Hillingdon from Suffolk in 1889, and my great uncle William set up in business as builder and undertaker in the premises where A.V. Smith & Sons are today. Apart from his work as a builder, William was a skilled wood-carver, and some of his work survives in St John's church.

William Buttrum's wood-carving workshop.

In November 1898 my grandparents and their children came from Suffolk to join their relations, and so my mother and some of her sisters attended the church girls' school in Royal Lane. The building has been the church hall since 1931, but it still looks like a school. My mother's memories included attending the church on Sunday mornings, when Lord and Lady Hillingdon were often to be seen in the front pew.

I am therefore more than grateful to Sutton Publishing for affording me the opportunity to place on record my findings and observations about the village in days gone by.

For over fifty years the Uxbridge Local History Society has been publishing the reminiscences of local residents, and sometimes just a few sentences have revealed a way of life in Hillingdon village that has now gone for ever.

In about 1896 Grace Young said, 'A balloon came down in the Glebe Field just at the side of the school, and we all ran out. It didn't come down on the ground, but came low enough for the men to talk to us. They wanted to know where they were, and we gave them the information One of the shopkeepers from the village was there by the time we'd finished telling them where they were, and the money they threw out, which I suppose was meant for the children, went into the man's pocket.'

Edith Musto and her sister Miriam Buttrum recalled, 'In the evenings our family used to watch the chairs coming through Hillingdon from Wycombe, piled up as high as they could be on horse-drawn vehicles on their way to town. Hay and straw would also come up from Amersham way, all bound for London. A four-in-hand coach plying between London and Oxford also used to come along, and you knew all about it when the man sitting at the back blew his long horn! The coach came from London one day, and returned the next, the horses being changed at the Red Lion each time.'

Violet Mitchell, speaking of a slightly later era, wrote, 'Each evening, as the light was failing, the tramps would walk into the village, and perhaps knowing it was too early, would sit down on the path to wait for the right time to go down to the Workhouse (where the Hospital now is). As children we found them rather frightening, because they were not well cared for, and they were rough. They would sit there, and perhaps go to sleep. We children were rather unkind to them, because we would go and stare at them but not talk to them.'

Arthur Gorham recalled that although the churchyard was closed for burials in new graves in 1867, burials continued until 1948 in family plots. As a child of about eight Arthur was involved in two burials in vaults. The vaults were brick-lined, and built to take six or eight coffins. When they were nearly full, it was the custom to send a child into the vault to pull the coffin into position as it was lowered. Arthur said, 'They chose the littlest child', and he was that child. He added that people liked to frighten small boys, and this they did by threatening to brick him in with the coffin in the vault.

My sincere hope is that my readers will enjoy what follows, and get an even fuller picture of life in Hillingdon village in times past.

K.R. Pearce, 2007

1

The Distant Past

The ancient earthwork that skirts Coney Green, shown here in 1967, may well point
to the Saxon origin of the settlement. The place-name Hillingdon, spelt 'Hillendone' in
the Domesday Book of 1086, means 'hill of a man named Hille'. It seems probable
that a small group of Saxon tribesmen arrived on the site, and threw up a defensive
bank around their camp. Over a thousand years later part of it survives, although
now obscured by trees.

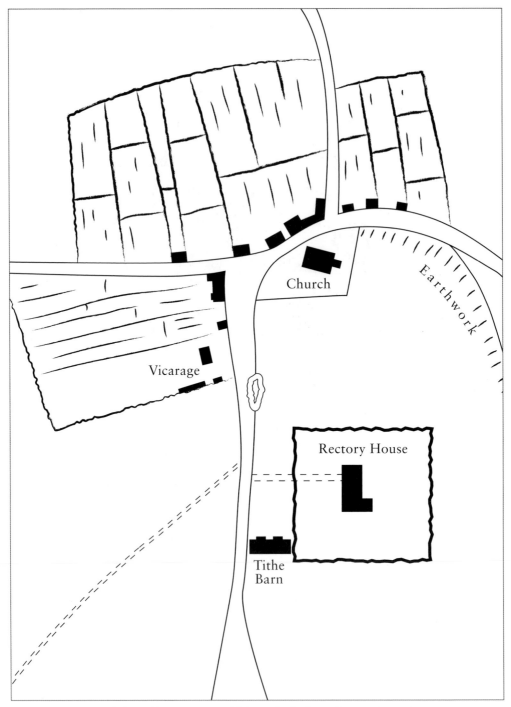

A reconstruction of the village as it would have looked in about 1300. The Saxon manor-house, surrounded by a ditch or moat, passed into the hands of the Bishop of Worcester in 1281. The bishop was now the rector of the parish, and was entitled to a tithe (one-tenth) of the produce. The church stands on a corner of the rectory land adjoining the main London to Oxford road. Beyond are the three fields divided into strips for the benefit of the villagers. This is a classic medieval English village.

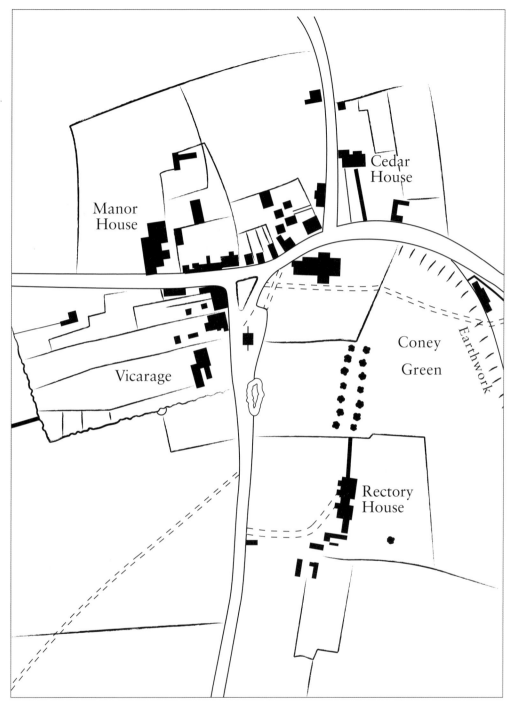

The same area in about 1870. The Rectory House has been twice rebuilt, and is about to be renamed Bishopshalt. The church and churchyard have both been enlarged, and shops and cottages now front the high road. The strip fields have long since disappeared, and two large houses are to be seen – the Cedar House, built in the reign of Elizabeth I, and the Manor House dating from about 1800. The area we know today is now recognisable.

About the year 1115 the manor of Hillingdon was given by Brian Fitzcount, the Norman lord, to the Abbey of Evesham. For well over a century the black-robed Benedictine monks settled in the former manor house, and Hillingdon became an outpost of the monastery. In the year 1281 the property was transferred to the Bishop of Worcester, and in 1283 bishop Godfrey Giffard came to stay in Hillingdon – the first bishop to halt here on his way to and from London. The effigy on bishop Giffard's tomb in Worcester Cathedral is shown here. The bishops owned this site until 1855.

Of the memorial brasses in the church, the finest is undoubtedly that of John, Lord Strange (d. 1479) and his wife Jacquetta, née Woodville. By this time the manors of Hillingdon and Colham had become joined, and Lord Strange was lord of the manor. This memorial brass was ordered by their daughter Joanna, who appears in miniature between her parents. Joanna married George Stanley, son of the first Earl of Derby. Jacquetta's sister Elizabeth became Queen of England when she married Edward IV.

This view of the village dates from 1717 and, although the work of an untrained artist, it gives us a valuable glimpse of life at the time. To the left of the church tower is the cedar tree that gave the Cedar House its name. The tree was one of the earliest cedars planted in this country, and was also one of the largest. In 1800 it was said to be 53ft high, and the girth of the trunk close to the ground was 15½ft. In front of the tree the sign of the Vine Inn juts across the road. Just to the right of the lych-gate are the village stocks (five holes!) and whipping post – a reminder of the harsh penalties for offenders in those days. A shaped yew tree stands in the churchyard, and the ladder used to carry out this topiary can be seen fixed to the wall of the church nearby. Behind the tree a string of washing is apparent! Just off to the right, and out of this drawing, stood some 'church cottages' or almshouses at this period. They were demolished in 1745, but in 1717 the occupants were using the churchyard as a drying area for their clothes.

The main road that passes through the village is the ancient London to Oxford road, and in the second half of the eighteenth century it became one of the main coaching roads of England. This painting of the Uxbridge coach by Henry J. Jones seems to show a stagecoach in Hillingdon, with the church on the left and the Red Lion inn on the right.

This property stood in Royal Lane to the south of Pield Heath Road, and was called The Cottage. This photograph was taken in 1928, and is a reminder that for centuries Hillingdon village lay in the pleasant countryside of West Middlesex. Memorials in the church and churchyard indicate that it was a rural area to which Londoners of substance liked to retire.

2

The Church of
St John the Baptist

The church tower, standing tall on the brow of Hillingdon Hill, is a landmark for miles around. It dates from 1629, when it was rebuilt to replace an earlier structure that had become unsafe. The previous tower was mentioned in the will of a certain Alice Yonge in 1404. The tower houses a fine peal of ten bells.

This drawing of 1836 shows the church from the north-east, with the original chancel on the left. By 1846 it became evident that the church was too small for the ever-increasing population, and so the eminent architect George Gilbert Scott was asked to prepare plans for an extension. The work was carried out in 1847/8 by the Uxbridge builders Messrs Fassnidge.

Throughout the 1890s this drawing appeared on the cover of the parish magazine, and clearly shows the additions made. The nave was extended, transepts were added, and the chancel with flanking chapels was built at the east end. The chapel on the left now houses the pipe organ, while the other is the Lady Chapel.

This view, similar to that of 1836, shows the north transept prominently in the foreground. A vestry has since been added on the north-east corner, and was ready in 1964. The turret on the tower houses the ancient curfew bell of the parish, still in use in the early years of the nineteenth century. The ringing of the bell was a signal that people should leave the streets and public places, and retire to their homes.

The chancel of St John's in the 1920s, showing the great east window above the altar, and the pulpit on the right. At this period the words of the ten commandments were painted on either side of the window, and these can just be detected today. The plain barrel roof shown here was thoroughly cleaned and painted in 1953 to commemorate the coronation of Queen Elizabeth II.

Another view of the chancel in about 1905, photographed by the then organist Louis Hamand. Mr Hamand later became organist of Malvern Priory, and his autobiography *An Organist Remembers* (1949) includes reminiscences of his days in Hillingdon. The elaborate handrail on the right, by the pulpit steps, has long since disappeared.

Church activities expanded in the second half of the nineteenth century, and the population continued to grow. Mission rooms were built at Colham Green (1872) and Hillingdon Heath (1884). The second of these, on the corner of the main road and Nellgrove Road, is shown here. By 1980 both had fallen out of use, and were sold. Today both survive, having undergone a change of use.

On the north side of the chancel is the fine memorial to Henry Paget, first Earl of Uxbridge. The Paget family lived in the manor house at West Drayton, of which only the gatehouse remains today. Henry was created Earl of Uxbridge in 1714, died in 1743 aged 83, and is shown here reclining in Roman dress. The sculptor was Louis Francois Roubiliac. The Earl left the people of Hillingdon £200, a sum which enabled them to build a parish workhouse at Colham Green. This workhouse has evolved into Hillingdon Hospital.

On the south side of the chancel is the fine alabaster monument to Sir Edward and Lady Jane Carr, who lived at the Rectory House (now Bishopshalt) in the early seventeenth century. The couple are shown kneeling on either side of a prayer-stool. The monument was paid for by their daughters Philadelphia and Jane, who are shown in the foreground holding hands. This memorial was damaged by a small bomb which fell just outside in 1940. Little Jane's head has been glued back on, but Lady Jane's nose was never repaired!

On the night of 8 November 1940 a small bomb fell on the south side of the church. Our photograph shows a window in the south aisle, with shattered glass and damaged stonework. Almost all the windows on the south and east sides were damaged, and a few destroyed. Replacement was carried out in the post-war period, but there remains an area of the churchyard where there are no gravestones.

Prebendary Charles Musgrave Harvey was vicar of St John's from 1895 to 1916. At this period, with the two mission rooms functioning, two curates were also working in the parish. In this photograph Charles Harvey is flanked by the Revd J.H. Wooster and the Revd A.J. Jones.

The Revd Robert Mallabar Carrick was vicar from 1916 to 1921.

The Revd Henry James Kitcat was the incumbent from 1921 to 1934.

The tomb of John Rich (1692?–1761), who lived latterly in the parish. His name will live for ever in the history of the English stage, for he ran the first Covent Garden Theatre in London, and introduced pantomime into this country. His home was at Cowley Grove, a large property in Cowley Road, Uxbridge. It was finally a hotel, and was demolished in 1967. (The houses in Frayslea are now on the site.)

Several tombstones in the churchyard bear the symbol of a skull and crossbones, like the one above, and they have evoked the fanciful idea that there are pirates buried there. The fact is that they are simply symbols of death, but it must be said that the local sculptor seems to have been skilled at that task. At one time coffins of well-to-do families were interred in vaults under the church floor, but in about 1805 Count Peter De Salis complained of 'the offensive smell I have repeatedly perceived'. The practice then ceased.

This tombstone, now fading, is of special interest. It reads, 'Here lieth Toby Pleasant. An African born, he was early in life rescued from West Indian slavery by a gentleman of this parish, which he ever gratefully remembered, and who he continued to serve as a Freeman, honestly and faithfully to the end of his life. He died 2nd May 1784, aged about 45 years.'

This little card has been enlarged, as it is only 3in wide. It once slotted into a small frame on a pew in the church, and is a reminder that at one time you could reserve a seat in the church each Sunday; the church derived income from these 'pew rents'. Archibald Frank Gotch (1872–1944) was senior master, i.e. deputy head, at Bishopshalt School from 1908 to 1937.

The old vicarage in Royal Lane, parts of which dated from the eighteenth century. The last vicar to live there, Prebendary Tyler, found it too large, out-dated and damp. He later wrote, 'The Georgian section was so damp, that if you left a briefcase there for a couple of weeks it would be covered by a cloud of mould.' The property was demolished in 1962, and replaced by a housing development called The Chantry. A new vicarage was found nearby.

Prebendary Frank Tyler and his wife Kathleen in the garden of the new vicarage. The photograph was taken in 1977, when Mr and Mrs Tyler, after twenty-eight years in the parish, were about to retire to Warminster. The detached house they occupied had been built in 1932 for John Miles, the headmaster of Bishopshalt School. With alterations, it remains the vicarage today.

3

The Road That Disappeared

Charville Lane in 1905, a rural corner of Hillingdon giving no hint that in an earlier age it had been part of a road from the village to Harrow – a road that was destined to largely disappear.

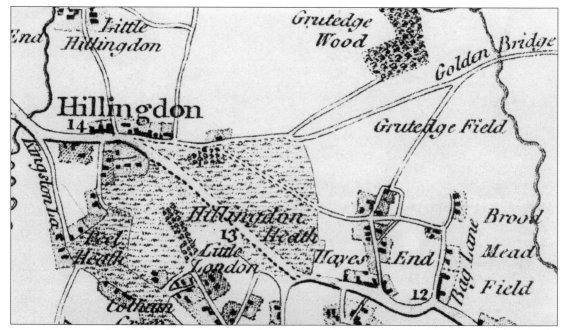

A section of Rocque's map shows the road clearly leaving Hillingdon, passing along the north side of the Heath, and on to the Golden Bridge. A number of houses can be seen between the village and Long Lane, but under the Enclosure Award of 1825 their front gardens were extended to the main road. This had the effect of cutting off the road, and it fell into disuse. Parts survive today as Charville Lane West, and Charville Lane as far as Golden Bridge. Beyond is a footpath leading to Sharvell Lane and West End Road.

Glenthorne in Uxbridge Road is one of the properties that once fronted the old road, which is why it appears now to have been built at an odd angle to the highway.

A little further eastward is Perryfield, built by William Perry (1747–1827) As a young naval doctor Perry went on Captain Cook's first voyage to the antipodes. He later ran a school in Edinburgh, and compiled at least four dictionaries. He retired to Hillingdon in about 1800, and he and his wife are buried in the churchyard.

The Grange boarded up and awaiting demolition in 1967. For many years it had been the home of Sir Gilfrid and Lady Craig, who were noted for their public service. Juliet Craig was a strong supporter of the Guide movement, and many rallies were held in the grounds here.

Wilton House was nearer Long Lane, and in 1950 was described as an 'imposing detached gentleman's residence standing in three and a half acres of matured grounds'. It was demolished in about 1970.

Hillingdon Place was next to Long Lane, and stood on a very large plot of land. It is said to have been built by an Admiral Drake in the eighteenth century, and was later occupied by the De Salis family. In the mid-1930s the developer Herbert Bayliss Silver acquired the estate. He built the shops called Crescent Parade, and several hundred houses behind it to the west of Long Lane.

4

Hillingdon Heath

Young Frank Rayner on his butcher's round before the First World War. The Heath
was still quite rural, though much of its 200 acres of open land had gone. In 1678
the coach of Sir Robert Vyner, who lived at Swakeleys, was stopped on the Heath by
eleven highwaymen, and the travellers were 'robbed and maltreated'. All eleven were
later arrested, and the ringleaders were hanged.

This postcard of part of the Heath was produced soon after the electric trams began to run in the summer of 1904, and an open-topped tramcar of the London United Tramways can be seen in the distance. The shops of Hall Terrace, on the left, remain there today.

The London United Tramways opened a tram depot and generating station opposite the entrance to New Road, and this was in use until 1922. The buildings were then taken by Compton's, a coachbuilding firm (shown here), and later still by Lang Wheels, a company that manufactured fairground equipment.

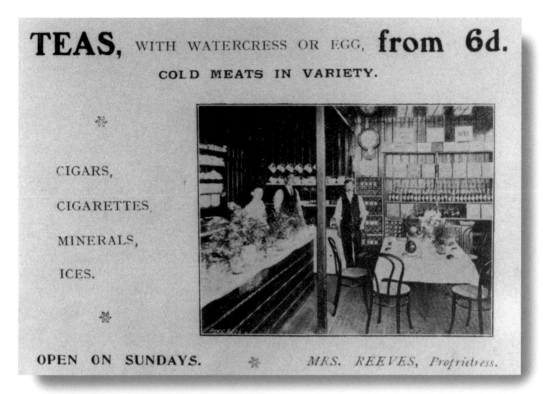

TEAS, WITH WATERCRESS OR EGG, **from 6d.**

COLD MEATS IN VARIETY.

CIGARS,

CIGARETTES,

MINERALS,

ICES.

OPEN ON SUNDAYS.   *MRS. REEVES, Proprietress.*

The trams brought Londoners out to West Middlesex, and Mrs. Reeves was soon advertising her Electric Refreshment Rooms opposite the generating station. Her customers could walk north to Charville Lane, or south to West Drayton, along the country roads and lanes.

One of the early developments on the Heath was the building of Salem Baptist Chapel in 1843, shown above on the left. Before this the members had met in a nearby cottage. In 1908 the building was replaced as a place of worship by the one on the right, still in use today. The old building was finally demolished in 1961, and a modern church hall, set back from the main road, replaced it. (*Salem Baptist Church*)

The Worley family pictured in the garden of their home in Charles Street, *c.* 1897. George Worley, second from left, ran a building business, and was one of the prominent characters of the district. With him are his father, John Caleb, his wife Sarah, and his children William, Thirza and Albert.

Barbara Miles with her four children in the garden of their home in New Road. The children are (from left) Leonard, Kathleen, Bernard and Enid. Young Bernard, holding his teddy bear, was born here in September 1907, and on leaving school he entered the acting profession. He appeared in many plays, films and television shows, and eventually founded the Mermaid Theatre in London. He was then elevated to the peerage as Lord Miles of Blackfriars.

These two pictures show some of the products of Henry Cripps' rustic furniture business in Butler Street. Garden seats, fencing, shelters and even an imitation wishing well feature among the items on sale – somehow very apt in these semi-rural surroundings. The firm continued to trade until about 1968.

The entrance to Long Lane seen from the main road in 1930. The entrance gate and lodge to Hillingdon Place are on the left, and just off the picture on the right was a small petrol filling-station. Within a very few years this scene was dramatically changed. The lane became a major road. The Crescent Parade shops rose on the left, and a larger garage was built on the right. Note the tram-lines in the main road.

Opposite the end of Long Lane today stands the Wonder Café, and here it is in its earliest days – a small wooden hut in 1933. Above it is a large sign advertising new homes off Long Lane priced at £450. Housing development along both sides of Long Lane was by then rapidly taking place.

Further east, near the Lees Road junction, ribbon development continued in 1935. Whiteley's, the London department store, had earlier had a nursery here to grow plants and flowers. After it closed the shops there were named Whiteley's Parade.

On 26 September 1940 a Nazi land-mine exploded in the Connaught Recreation Ground, and many nearby homes were damaged. The turret of the Mission Room can be seen here in the background. Several people were injured, but none seriously.

In the late afternoon of 28 January 1941 a bomb destroyed the assembly hall at Hillingdon Primary School. Most of the children had gone home, and those that remained were in the air-raid shelters. The only casualty was school attendance officer Reginald Anscombe, who was standing in the entrance to the shelter. He sustained severe head injuries, and died four days later in Hillingdon Hospital.

A glimpse of the young Bernard Miles, third from left, already showing promise as an actor at Uxbridge County School in the Greenway in 1924. The other boys are (from left) F.E. Smith, Bernard's older brother Leonard, and Hugh Mansford. They had performed a scene from Shakespeare's *King John*.

Earlier Bernard had attended Hillingdon Primary School, and in December 1948 he returned as a distinguished ex-pupil to make a retirement presentation to the headmaster, Mr. Murphy. By then Bernard had appeared in notable films such as *In Which We Serve* and David Lean's *Great Expectations*.

5

Vine Lane

The lane takes its name from the public house on the main road, and when this photograph was taken in about 1930 it still had a remarkably rural look. House-building was about to begin here on both sides of the road.

A view from before the First World War showing an early motor car emerging from a dip in the lane. At one time water ran across the road at the lowest point, but no longer. The building of houses has completely altered the natural drainage system.

In 1892 an area to the west of Vine Lane, part of the Hillingdon House estate, became Hillingdon Golf Club. The founders were Charles Newton, who lived at Hillingdon House, a local solicitor named John Hibbert, and Charles Stevens who was a partner in an Uxbridge timber firm. Today the club continues to flourish on the same site. (Hillingdon Golf Club)

Queen Victoria's staghounds meeting in the grounds of Hillingdon House in 1848. The first house on the site was built by the Duke of Schomberg in 1727, but it was destroyed by fire in 1844. This print shows the recently completed second house built for the owner, Richard Henry Cox. He was a partner in a London bank, Cox & Co., specialising in the accounts of army officers.

Another view of Hillingdon House, this time from a sale brochure of 1913 when the Cox family had decided to sell their Hillingdon House and Harefield Place estates. The Government acquired Hillingdon House in 1915.

Another view from the 1913 brochure showing the house in its parkland setting, and a lake formed by widening the River Pinn. A large orangery is to be seen in the distance on the right. The Royal Flying Corps, later RAF, occupied the estate in 1917 and it was initially their Armament and Gunnery School.

In 1825 Mr (later Sir) Charles Mills (1792–1872), who had married Richard Cox's daughter
Emily, purchased a house on the east side of Vine Lane. He was a partner in another City
bank, Glyn Mills & Co., and had inherited a considerable fortune. At that period the family
owned a villa on the Palatine Hill in Rome, where this portrait was drawn.

Charles Mills was later able to buy an adjacent property, and he decided to demolish them both and build a brand new mansion. He employed the architect Philip Charles Hardwick, and the result was Hillingdon Court, shown here. It was completed in about 1855, and by 1861 Mills and ten members of his family were living there, looked after by thirty-three servants.

Another aspect of Hillingdon Court. In 1886 Sir Charles Mills (1830–98), son of the Charles already mentioned, was created Baron Hillingdon for political and public services. He began to expand the Hillingdon estate by purchasing farms and other property that came on the market. The area eventually amounted to 3,185 acres, and gave Lord Hillingdon the extensive shooting grounds that he desired.

By 1918 the health of the second Lord Hillingdon (1855–1919) had deteriorated, and he had purchased this horse-drawn invalid carriage to take him round the grounds of Hillingdon Court. Lady Hillingdon, seen here holding the reins, was the Hon. Alice Harbord, daughter of Baron Suffield. After Lord

Hillingdon's death the entire estate was put on the market. Within a few years hundreds of houses were built in what became known as North Hillingdon.

The Hillingdon Court mansion was bought by the Roman Catholic order of the Sacred Heart of Mary, and it became a nursing home for elderly residents. In October 1940 seven small bombs fell on the house and grounds. One made a hole in a bedroom wall (as shown) but the lady in bed there was completely unharmed because it failed to explode. She then announced to staff that it was time she went to the air-raid shelter!

In an inner courtyard of the mansion was the well that had supplied water to the household for decades. Another bomb fell straight down the well-shaft, and exploded at the bottom. The water-filled crater is shown here; that was the end of the well! In the post-war years the mansion became a Convent School for girls, catering for boarding and day pupils. It closed in 1977.

In 1978 Hillingdon Court was purchased by the American Community Schools organisation, and their International School flourishes there today under the head of school, Mrs Ginger G. Apple. The six hundred pupils, whose ages range from four to nineteen, come from about forty different countries. One fixture in the summer is the Graduation Ceremony for school leavers. Wearing caps and gowns they receive their diplomas and awards. Finally, in a burst of jubilation, they throw their caps high in the air, as shown here. *(ACS International School)*

This house in Vine Lane, formerly known as Fives Court, was designed and lived in from 1928 by the self-styled 'psychological architect' Grace Cope (1873–1947). The windows at roof level are in her 'disgruntling room', a place of retreat in times of stress. Miss Cope also designed Stewartby next door, which was ready in 1929.

6

The Village

A view of the village in 1898. The Vine Inn, on the extreme right, offered food and accommodation for travellers. The Red Lion Inn is just visible beyond the tree in the distance. As yet there is no proper surface on the highway between London and Uxbridge.

James Bunce (1788–1865) stands at the door of his cottage in the main street. He was the village blacksmith, and his forge was situated at the back of the Red Lion. In his prime he was 6ft 2in tall, and weighed 23 stone. He always wore knee breeches, buckled shoes and a broad-rimmed hat. When fire broke out at Hillingdon House in 1844 he is said to have carried out a piano single-handed. During his 77 years he never slept away from this cottage in which he had been born.

Hillingdon Cricket Club can trace its origins back to about 1834, which makes it one of the oldest clubs in the area. For almost all that time Coney Green has been their home ground. In this 1896 team photograph are, back row, left to right: H. Bunce, G. Dudley, F. Bunce, L. Hedges, A. Bragg (scorer). Middle row: A. Youens, S. Tyrell, W. Bellamy, F. Youens. Front row: W. Weeden, E. Cowdery (umpire), S. Weedon. In January 2006 the club merged with Ruislip Manor Cricket Club, and now plays at Coney Green under the name Hillingdon Manor Cricket Club.

Hillingdon Football Club also played on Coney Green, and this photograph of the team and officials dates from a very successful 1898/99 season. The players are, back row, left to right: H. Hedges, D. Miles, E. Ayres. Middle row: W. Richardson, A. Mitchell, T. Richardson. Front row: W.G. Smith, A. Bailey, E. Hedges, E. Miles, R. Richardson. The club's linesman, A.J. Pratt, is holding his flag.

44   Hillingdon—Advertisements.

FREDERICK LILLEY,

Corn, Coal & Coke Merchant,

CONTRACTOR & CARMAN,

Opposite the Church, Hillingdon.

ALL COALS DOUBLE SCREENED.

Every description of light work done. Furniture removed to all parts.

WM. BUTTRUM,

✦ BUILDER, ✦

HILLINGDON HILL, NEAR UXBRIDGE.

PAINTING & DECORATING.

FURNITURE MADE AND REPAIRED.

All kinds of Sanitary Work executed on the latest improved principles.

ESTIMATES GIVEN FOR GENERAL REPAIRS.

Some advertisements from the local directory in the year 1895. Before the electric trams appeared in 1904 people did not travel far, and almost everything you wanted could be obtained in or near the village.

ESTABLISHED 1874.

✦H. J. PENN,✦

Upholsterer and Bedding Manufacturer,

HILLINGDON HEATH.

**SOFAS, COUCHES AND EASY CHAIRS
RESTUFFED AND COVERED.**

Window Blinds of all kinds made & fixed to order.

MATTRESSES RE-MADE EQUAL TO NEW.

H.J.P. desires to return his sincere thanks for the liberal patronage bestowed on him during the past year, and begs to state that he will use every endeavour to give entire satisfaction in each department of his business.

✦JAMES HEDGES,✦

TAILOR,

THE VILLAGE, HILLINGDON.

LIVERIES, &c., MADE ON THE MOST LIBERAL TERMS.   PARISH CLERK.

W. RATCLIFF,

BREAD * AND * BISCUIT * BAKER,

OPPOSITE THE CHURCH, HILLINGDON.

Genuine Home-baked Bread   Groats, Oatmeal, Split Peas and Bird Seeds.

ESTABLISHED 1878.   **A. HAINES,**

GENERAL DRAPER, Stationery and Fancy Stores,

6, Hall Terrace, Hillingdon.

Agent for the London Drug Store, and Campbell & Co.'s Dye Works, Perth.

More advertisements from 1895. A visit to the larger shops in the town of Uxbridge would have been regarded as a treat at this period – especially by the children.

Alexander Mitchell (1847–1905) is seen here at the door of his saddlery shop. Alex took the store over in 1873, and ran it until his death. As a side-line he sold honey produced by his own bees. He served on Hillingdon Parish Council, and was prominent in local affairs. He was one of the ringleaders when, in 1897, a gang of villagers unblocked and cleared a footpath at the east end of Charville Lane. It had been closed by Lord Hillingdon a few years earlier.

The same premises in 1933, when it had become Clarke's general store, but also offering 'teas and refreshments'. On the right are large hoardings advertising the films at the RAF and Savoy cinemas in Uxbridge. A short section of the Cedar House wall is on the left. Road widening in the 1950s led to the demolition of this property.

William Buttrum (1859–1929) set up in business in the village as a builder and undertaker in about 1890, and occupied the premises now trading as A.V. Smith & Sons. Here we see Mr Buttrum and his employees preparing to go on a day trip to Marlow in the summer of 1908.

William Buttrum's workshops at the rear of his premises. Many years later the large building was converted into offices, and was demolished in 2003 when the Red Lion was considerably enlarged to become a hotel.

Photographs from the Buttrum family album showing costume of about 1900. Clockwise from top left: William and his eldest son Frederick; his daughters Evelyn, Ellen and Edith; his sons Alfred and Albert; his son Cyril in naval uniform.

Hillingdon Church and Village, Uxbridge

When I am sad and lonely, this is where I go.

The church is seen neatly framed between two trees – an oak on the left and an elm on the right. The date on the postmark of this card is August 1904.

The elm again, in front of Elm Tree Cottage, and Royal Lane on the right. It is said that the house was built for Miss Mills, sister of Lord Hillingdon, but she never lived in it. Instead she moved to Devon in 1896. The magnificent elm tree became the victim of dutch elm disease in the summer of 1975.

The Cedar House dates from the reign of Queen Elizabeth I, and is now a Grade II listed building. A botanist named Samuel Reynardson lived here from 1678 to 1721, and planted one of the first cedars ever to appear in England. When the tree was removed following storm damage in 1789, the girth of the trunk 3½ft above the ground was 13ft 6in. It is from this gigantic tree that the house takes its name. The first-floor room where Oliver Cromwell stayed is still identified, and the house later became the home of his grandson Major General Richard Russell. During the Second World War the house was commandeered by the army, and then from 1951 to 1970 it housed Rutland House Preparatory School. The property was then restored by Shephard Hill & Co., civil engineers, who received a Civic Trust award for their work. The house is now converted to office accommodation.

The Cottage, shown here in 1954, dates from the mid-sixteenth century, but has later additions. In the early part of the twentieth century it was the home of Christopher Stone (1882–1965), writer and broadcaster, who in 1925 founded a magazine called *The Gramophone* with his brother-in-law Compton Mackenzie, the novelist. The house later became a hotel, but in 2003 it was absorbed into the Red Lion, and has lost its separate identity.

Hillingdon Fair originated on 16 May 1372, when the villagers celebrated the granting of a chantry by King Edward III. (This was an endowment to cover expenses in saying daily prayers for the souls of the departed.) In the nineteenth century the fair changed from being a village celebration into an event run by fairground operators, and in the twentieth century it moved from the main road into Coney Green. This picture was taken in 1993, five years before the last fair was held. (*The World's Fair*)

The arrival of the electric trams in June 1904 had a great impact on the village, and here we see workmen checking the new rails. There was concern that the clanking of the trams would disturb worship in St John's church, so near the church the rails were laid in wooden blocks instead of stone setts.

An open-topped tram of the London United Tramways passes the Red Lion on its way to Shepherds Bush. Large numbers of cyclists were now coming out from London at weekends, and the emblem of the Cyclists Touring Club is on the wall beneath the lamp. In 1903 Ann Ashton, who weighed 20 stone, died in an upstairs room, and her body could not be manoeuvred down the narrow staircase. It was therefore passed out of the window on to the hearse waiting below.

KING'S "GAZETTE" ALMANACK, 1904.

M. J. NEWMAN,

Baker & Confectioner,

Corn, Forage and

Seed Merchant,

High Street, HILLINGDON.

Wedding Cakes made to order.

JOHN BUCKELDEE,

REGISTERED PLUMBER,

 ## HILLINGDON VILLAGE.

ELECTRIC LIGHT INSTALLATIONS.

Baths, W.C.'s, &c., fixed on the most modern Systems. Advice, Specifications and Estimates Free for every description of Hot and Cold Water Fitting and Sanitary Work.

DRAINS TESTED AND REPORTED ON.

Approved Plumber by the Rickmansworth and Uxbridge Valley Water Company.

WORK DONE FOR THE TRADE.

A. MITCHELL,

SADDLER & HARNESS MAKER,

HILLINGDON.

BEE KEEPER.

Prize Medallist at the Colonial Exhibition, 1886.

PURE HONEY ON SALE.

The 1904 advertisement of John Buckledee heralds another change. Electricity was now being generated in a works in Waterloo Road, Uxbridge, and lighting could be installed in people's homes. Piped water had also arrived. Mr Buckledee's son, also John, later became a partner in Buckledee and Tayler, an Uxbridge electrical firm.

Matthew Newman (1862–1943) worked in the family bakery business for sixty years, finally retiring in 1931. He sang in St John's church choir, and played for Hillingdon Cricket Club as a young man.

The death of 23-year-old Alf Buttrum following an incident in a football match in 1910 caused much public consternation. Alf's leg was scratched by a rusty buckle on an opponent's shinguard, and lockjaw set in. At that time there was no cure. 'Tiddler' Buttrum, as he was called because of his lack of height, was a popular player with Uxbridge FC, and his funeral was held on a Saturday afternoon. Football games for miles around were postponed, and crowds flocked to St John's church. Every home and shop had blinds drawn, or black boards placed at the windows. Prebendary Harvey conducted the funeral, his voice shaking with emotion. 'Many of the footballers were sobbing like little children', reported the local paper. This illustration is a postcard produced by Uxbridge FC in aid of the Buttrum Memorial Fund.

The village post office was taken over in 1919 by Mrs Lily Walmsley, and it was a busy life. Opening hours were 8 a.m. to 7 p.m. on weekdays, with the exception of Wednesday when they closed at 1 p.m. They even opened on Sunday mornings between 8.30 and 10 a.m. 'for telegrams and stamps only'. In this photograph we see Mrs Walmsley's daughter standing in the shop doorway. Her husband was the chief engineer at the Workhouse (later Hillingdon Hospital).

A scene in the village in 1933. The Red Lion is on the left, and the once-mighty oak tree is in the foreground. It is clear that at some time before this the tree had been savagely lopped, an act which appalled many at the time. One angry resident went so far as to nail a placard to the trunk bearing the one word 'Ichabod'. This is a Biblical word that means 'The glory has departed'. Behind the tree are the Hillcrest Tea Rooms (with own bakery) and a grocery store, but a road widening scheme meant that their days were numbered.

Milk being delivered in the village from Frederick Bunce's dairy, *c.* 1930. As yet bottles had not been introduced, so the milk was ladled into a jug or other container on the doorstep. Fred's sons Jack and Fred kept the dairy going until 1957, when they sold out to Express Dairies and retired. Their headed notepaper is shown below.

∷∷∷∷ F. BUNCE ∷∷∷∷

Pure Rich Milk
Fresh Cream Daily
Delicious Butter

Under
Personal
Supervision

DAIRY FARMER

Hillingdon Hill Farm Dairy, HILLINGDON, Middx.

Two scenes taken on the same day in 1930 are shown on this page. Prominent among the shops on the left are the village newsagent and Newman's bakery. In the distance the great cedar tree protrudes behind the Vine Inn. That tree, said to be a seedling from the original, still stands today, but is wired up to prevent damage from snow and ice.

The narrow entrance to Vine Lane, lit by a small gas-lamp, is on the right of this photograph. Beyond the Vine the canopy of the local butcher's shop straddles the pavement. In the distance a tramcar approaches, having just passed the Red Lion.

A last look at the village from the top of the hill in 1934. The houses and shops on the left are about to be swept away in the road widening programme. Our picture emphasises what a sharp bend there was in the main road as it curved to pass the church.

The full extent of the demolition is revealed in this 1935 scene, with the rubble of the old buildings not completely cleared. Yet already the new shops on the left are trading.

The old and the new Vine Inn are shown in these pictures of 1933 and 1935. Remarkably the gas-lamp on the corner of Vine Lane has survived the transformation. The Cannon Brewery Company financed the new public house, and they employed William Lionel Eves, an Uxbridge architect, to design the building. The Uxbridge builders Fassnidge & Son did the construction.

No. 607 trolleybuses replaced the trams in 1936, and this scene of about 1950 shows one of these vehicles passing the church. Once again the giant cedar tree is visible.

The trolleybuses were themselves replaced by Routemaster buses in November 1960, and here in July of that year we see pupils from Bishopshalt School queueing at the top of the hill on their way home.

7

Hillingdon Hill

From the tower of St John's church we look down on Hillingdon Hill, *c.* 1925.
A double-decker bus, with curved staircase at the rear, has passed the Red Lion and is
about to be concealed by the huge trees that line the hill-side. A field of Bunce's farm
is visible on the left. One might expect to see Uxbridge in the distance, but in fact the
road veers off sharply at the foot of the hill, and the town is well away to the right of
the picture.

This card is postmarked December 1912, and shows an open-topped tram climbing the hill. The upper deck was not the place to be in inclement weather, and the tram-driver himself had no cab or windscreen to protect him from the elements. At this time the fare from Uxbridge to Hillingdon village was one penny.

A view looking up the hill, with the cemetery gatehouse on the right. This entrance and two chapels were designed by a noted architect named Benjamin Ferrey, and were built by Messrs Fassnidge & Son of Uxbridge at a cost of £1,800. They were ready in February 1867.

One of the chapels designed by Ferrey. One was meant for Church of England burials, and the second for other denominations. Nowadays there are very few services at the cemetery, so one of the chapels is now a store used by the gardeners who work there. Near the east chapel is the headstone of Edward Stretton (d. 1871), who fought with the 2nd Life Guards at the battle of Waterloo.

The gatehouse and archway seen from inside the cemetery. The materials used in building these structures were described as 'Kentish rag with Bath Box-ground dressings and plain red tiles.'

The tree-lined hill
taken in 1930. For
most of the hill's
length the tram-lines
were single track,
hence the signal on
the right of the
picture. The vehicle
in the distance is
passing the cemetery
entrance on its way
uphill.

By the early 1930s the hill was becoming congested with traffic, and Middlesex County Council embarked on a scheme to create a new 'up' carriageway on the north side. Land was purchased, and the contractor, G. Percy Trentham, began work early in 1934. The project was completed the following year. These photographs show the work in progress in June 1934.

At the top of the hill on the north side stood the Manor House, shown here. It was built in about 1800, and for many years was the home of a family called Heming. The estate was acquired by builder R.T. Warren, who demolished the house in 1930 and redeveloped the site.

By 1935 the dual carriageway was finished, the main road through the village had been widened, and a row of new shops had appeared near where the Manor House had stood. The shops were aptly called Manor Parade, and boasted a sub-post office.

The top of the hill in 1935 after the completion of the dual carriageway. Warren houses are being built on the slope of the hill. Trams continued to use the old hill, but not for long. New vehicles called trolleybuses were about to be introduced.

Most of the Manor House grounds were developed by R.T. Warren as The Rise housing estate, shown here nearing completion. Some were detached with a garage, and cost about £800. Some had pleasant views across the golf course from their back windows.

The Fairway was part of The Rise estate, the name being inspired by the adjacent golf links. Robert Warren was a keen golfer and a member of Hillingdon Golf Club. Thanks to his generosity the club acquired a brand new clubhouse in 1931.

Here is The Crossway just completed. The Manor House stood about here, and so one resident today has the well in his garden which once supplied the mansion with water. Houses on the estate were advertised with the slogan, 'Come and live in healthy Hillingdon.'

At the foot of the hill the River Pinn runs under Stratford Bridge. (Stratford is usually thought to derive from the Old English word for 'ford on a Roman road'.) There was a sharp bend at this point, as our photograph shows, but in 1965 it was decided to widen the bridge to reduce the curve in the highway.

Here, in May 1967, we see the work in progress, The outcome is now that people drive past without realising that there is a bridge there at all. Few people today, if questioned, could tell you where Stratford Bridge is. According to the parish burial registers two men were murdered by the bridge in November 1702. One was Will Harrison, a 'penny postman', and the other Edward Symonds, a drover from Thame in Oxfordshire.

8

Royal Lane

A view from about 1930, with the Bishopshalt fence on the right. In the centre is Elm Tree Cottage, and beyond it some of the buildings in the main road. The lane supposedly takes its name from King Charles I, who is said to have lunched in the Red Lion in 1645, and then afterwards strolled down here with his chaplain and a groom.

St John's church hall was built in 1869 as a parish school for girls, and the house on the left was occupied by the headteacher. A reorganisation of local schools in 1928 saw the girls join the boys on Hillingdon Heath. (This is now Hillingdon Primary School.) The vacant building was then converted into a parish hall, and was opened in October 1931. Despite this, it still looks like a school.

The top class of girls at this school, *c.* 1905. They would have been thirteen or fourteen years old at the time of this photograph, and were about to leave. Back row, left to right: Annie Harding, Dorothy Stevens, Kate Mansfield, Gladys Williams, Christine Ballinger, Nellie Blower, Nellie Barfoot. Third row: Edith Carpenter, Nellie Gorham, M Tuckwell, Grace Hazell, Grace Cox. Second row: Eva Batcock, Nellie Harper, Eva Mitcham, Mabel Hearn, Rose Shepherd, Florrie Perkins, Daisy Brill. Front row: Nellie Crouchman, Winnie Allen, Nelly Lavender, Katie Fisher, Edith Buttrum.

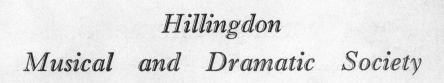

Hillingdon
Musical and Dramatic Society

PRESENT

(By permission of R. D'Oyly Carte, Esq.)

President—
Rev. H. J. KITCAT, M.A.

Vice-Presidents—
F. ALDIS, Esq.
L. BIRD, Esq.
Mrs. L. BIRD
T. S. BOLTON, Esq.
W. CATHERWOOD, Esq.
H. S. COX, Esq.
A. V. CRUMP, Esq.
R. A. CRUMP, Esq.
R. ETHERIDGE, Esq., B.A.
A. F. GOTCH, Esq.
—. HURST, Esq.
Mrs. HURST
Clr. W. E. MADDOCK
M. NEWMAN, Esq.
Clr. Mrs. M. E. O'DELL
G. PEDDLE, Esq.
G. STEPHENSON, Esq.
Sqdn. Ldr. H. STEELE
Clr. A. THORNLEY
Mrs. A. THORNLEY

Written by
W. S. GILBERT

Composed by
ARTHUR SULLIVAN

———

In Two Acts

AT ST. JOHN'S HALL
November 5th, 9th, 10th, 11th & 12th
at 8 p.m.

The church hall immediately became a popular venue for amateur stage productions, and in particular for the Hillingdon Musical and Dramatic Society, formed in 1928. We show the cover of a programme from about 1938, when the show was produced and conducted by Harold Stoddart. (Mr Stoddart was also headmaster of Cowley St Laurence School.)

The hall was also the home for many years of Hillingdon Women's Institute, which started up in February 1919, and is the oldest branch in Middlesex. To celebrate their seventieth anniversary the members planted a tree in the newly opened Stockley Park. Members shown include Doris Smith (president), Barbara Moulder, Joan MacIntosh, Celia Callard, Joyce Thomson, Louise Burn and Gladys Young. *(Hillingdon Women's Institute)*

Hidden away from view in the Lane is Tudor Cottage, a fine detached mock-Tudor residence built in 1926 by Milton Hutchings, the proprietor of a horticultural nursery off Pield Heath Road. (That nursery is now a garden centre.)

Travelling south from the village one encounters a sharp bend in the Lane, as the road avoids the former Grove Estate. This 1941 photograph shows the bend, and a footpath on one side of the Lane only. Part of Bishopshalt School can be seen on the right. Fred Bunce's cows grazed in a field behind the hedge on the left.

The Grove probably dated from the sixteenth century, and for a long period it belonged to the family of Lord Boston. One of the last owners was George Shawyer, a partner in the vast Lowe and Shawyer cut-flower nursery. Mr Shawyer added the sun lounge to the south of the property. The house was demolished in 1970, and the apartments of Robinwood Grove now occupy the site.

These two photographs were taken in 1962, and show a very rural scene. They are cottages in Grove Lane, and were probably built for workers on the Grove Estate. In recent years all these cottages have been replaced by modern houses.

9

Bishopshalt School

The school occupies an estate which belonged to the Bishops of Worcester for 574 years (see also page 10). The Middlesex Education Committee purchased the estate in 1925 for £6900, and this photograph was taken while alterations and extensions were being made to enable the school to transfer here. As Uxbridge County School, it had been founded in the Greenway, Uxbridge, in 1907.

The house which formed the nucleus of the estate is certainly the third and probably the fourth house to occupy the site. The present mansion was built in 1858 by John Jackson, a partner in a London building firm that specialised in plasterwork and interior decoration. Jackson lived here for only three years, and the property changed hands frequently in the Victorian era. This print was produced by a London firm of estate agents in 1886 when the property was on the market. It sold for £9,000.

These two drawings date from about 1800, and show the house that pre-dated the present one. It was built in about 1610, belonged to the Bishops of Worcester, and was known as the Rectory House. It was let to tenants, the last of whom was William Dry, who ran a boarding school for boys from about 1835 to 1855. The 1841 census shows twenty-one boarders, with ages ranging from seven to seventeen. Bishopshalt was not the first school on the site!

John Jackson demolished the Rectory House, built the present mansion, and totally relaid the gardens and grounds. He also had a lodge built at the main gate, shown here, which became the caretaker's house when the school moved to the site in 1928.

The last private owner of Bishopshalt was William Frederick Thomas (1829–1920). He had owned a factory in Clerkenwell manufacturing sewing machines, and in 1890 retired to this Hillingdon home having added several rooms on the south side. The only known photograph shows him on his yacht, the *Vacuna*. (*International Sewing Machine Collectors' Society*)

A look at Uxbridge County School in the Greenway in 1928, just as the move was taking place. For twenty-one years these premises had been the school's first home, but now they were inadequate for the large number of pupils, and adjacent land was not then available. Today these buildings form part of Uxbridge High School.

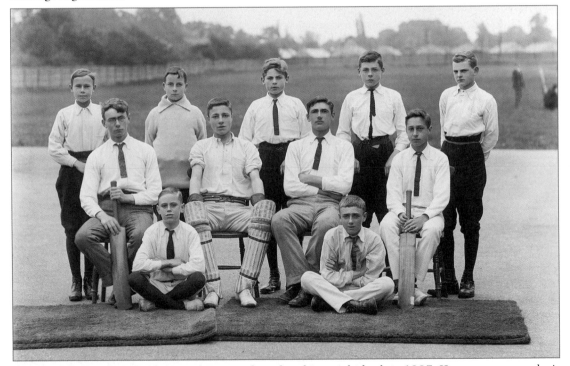

Despite the move the school retained its records and archives right back to 1907. Here, as an example, is a photograph of a House cricket team from 1910. Back row, left to right: William Umpleby, Harry Hartnoll, Charles Ward, Reginald Brie, Ernest Odell. Middle row: Lovell Cocks, Arthur Cole, Harry Perkins, George Thurlow. Front row: Donald Hall, Reginald Pratt.

Uxbridge County School moved to Hillingdon Village in the summer holidays of 1928, and was officially opened on 6 October by Sir John (later Lord) Reith, the director general of the BBC. Here Sir John, surrounded by dignitaries, is seen making his speech.

The above ceremony took place in the new assembly hall, but unfortunately the barrel ceiling proved an acoustic disaster. No solution has ever been found. Today it is the school's dining hall, and is also used for PE lessons.

The school was fortunate to inherit an ornamental garden complete with lily pond, croquet lawn and a wide variety of trees – much as John Jackson had intended. The two teachers pictured here are Agnes Black, who taught mathematics from 1918 to 1956, and Albert Walter, handicraft master from 1921 to 1946.

There had been no gymnasium in the Greenway premises, so there was great excitement to find this fully equipped room for Physical Training (as it was then called). A wood and glass partition, shown in the background, could be slid back so that the gymnasium became an extension to the assembly hall. This did not help the acoustics!

The headmaster was Walter Wilks Sawtell (1867–1948), who had held the post from the school's foundation. 'Billy' Sawtell also sought ordination in the Church of England, and in 1921 he became an assistant priest in Uxbridge. After seeing the school settled in its new home, he resigned in 1929 to become rector of Madehurst in Sussex.

Sir Cecil Fane De Salis (1857–1948) was involved with the school even before it opened. As a local representative on the Middlesex Education Committee he was one of two men asked in 1904 to find a suitable site for the new secondary school. He was appointed Chairman of the Governors from the start, and continued to take a close interest in the school for the rest of his life. His sons Edmund and Jerome became pupils. Until 1929 he and his family lived at Dawley Court in south Hillingdon, but they then moved to Wargrave.

Uxbridge County School was no longer in Uxbridge, and in 1930 it was resolved to change the school's name to Bishopshalt School. An approach was made to the College of Heralds to create a coat-of-arms, and the result was a pictorial version of the two names of the school. The triangle was an element of the arms of Uxbridge, and the Saxon swords, or seaxes, were part of the arms of the County of Middlesex. A bishop's mitre was joined by nine roundels from the arms of Worcester Cathedral. The full description is: Or, on a pile gules between nine torteaux, two seaxes in saltire proper pommels and hilts or, surmounted by a bishop's mitre or.

The School Song.

(Words by Mrs. De Salis. *Music by the late* J. H. Major.)

In days of old our Fathers fought
   On land and sea in England's cause,
Their battles o'er, their homes they sought
   And helped to frame our noble laws.

     Our Fathers served Old England,
     And we will serve her too.
     We'll work for her,
     We'll fight for her,
     And to her cause be true.

We know the deeds they did of yore
   And hope, one day, to do the same,
To serve our country more and more
   And leave behind an honour'd name.

     Our Fathers died for England,
     For Faith and Freedom too,
     We'll live for them,
     We'll die for them,
     To God and King be true.

When we have enter'd on life's task,
   We'll not forget what now we sing ;
And higher guerdon will not ask,
   Than for our School great fame to win.

     Then we will serve Old England,
     In countries old and new,
     We'll keep our Faith,
     And serve our race,
     And to our School be true.

In about 1909 Mrs Rachel De Salis, wife of the chairman of the governors, composed this school song, and the organist at St John's church set it to music. It was sung with patriotic gusto at school functions, but its use declined in the 1930s.

In July 1931 a Cierva autogyro landed on the school playing field. An autogyro was a propeller-driven light aircraft fitted with free-moving rotor blades to give near-vertical movement. The pilot was Reginald Brie (1895–1989), who had been one of the school's first pupils (see page 94). Brie later switched to helicopters, and is regarded as the pioneer of rotary-wing flying in Britain. Tennis and cricket matches between past and present pupils were being played, and a large crowd saw this notable event.

In the centre of this photograph is headmaster John Miles wearing a rosette. To his left are A.F. Gotch and Miss Margaret Kennedy-Bell, who had both taught Brie. Next is Brie himself. On the left are head prefects Marjorie Minett and Ralph Hadley. On the right in striped blazers are former pupils Olive Smith and W.H. Kennedy.

The value of the ornamental garden as a setting for open-air drama was soon recognised, and here is a scene from the 1933 production of *A Midsummer Night's Dream*. Drama teacher Cecilia Hill was the producer.

Although the school had changed its name the old pupils' association did not, and to this day they are still known as the Old Uxonians. Their Dramatic Club was very active between the wars, and here is the cast of Emlyn Williams' play *A Murder Has Been Arranged*, staged in St John's Hall in 1932. The players included W.H. Kennedy (producer), Nora Pullen, Daisy Williams, Eunice Carden, Molly Cowan, A.C. Simmonds, Constance Lyons, C.J. Tolley and Brian Trant.

A paperchase was an annual event at this period. Two boys, the 'hares', were sent out with satchels full of torn-up paper, and they laid a trail to be followed by the 'hounds'. In 1930 the 'hares' were Freddie Alford (left) and Ralph Hadley. Alford later became managing director of the Uxbridge printing and stationery firm of Perry and Routleff. Hadley became sports editor of the *People* newspaper.

Here are the 'hounds' leaving the school gate in pursuit, much to the delight of the watching girls who are not involved. The area was sufficiently rural, and the traffic sufficiently light, to make this event viable – but not for much longer!

The school's first stage musical, *The Mikado*, was performed in St John's Hall in 1936 under the baton of Myfanwy Butler. The cast consisted of past and present pupils, as well as teaching staff. Here are the principals. Back row, left to right: Charles Hutchings, Leonard Clarke, Benjamin Butler, William Jackson (producer), Ella Williams and 'Ken' Kennedy. Front row: Marie Gale, Mary Polwart, Betty Tapping.

The growth of Nazi dominance in Europe in the 1930s eventually prompted the government to prepare for war, and in September 1938 the population was issued with gas-masks. This is the boys' cloakroom at Bishopshalt on the day of issue. On every peg hangs a school cap and a gas-mask.

War came in 1939, and with it the resolve to help the war effort in every possible way. Here is a party of lads camping at a farm at Missenden in Buckinghamshire, and helping to bring in the harvest in the late summer of 1942. Teachers with the party are 'Billy' Butler (second from left) and 'Whacker' Davies (extreme right).

A rally and inspection of the local branch of the Girls' Training Corps was held in the hard playground in the summer of 1943. At this period there was still evidence of the once-private Bishopshalt estate, for the playground was originally a walled garden. On the walls can be seen the whitewash of the former greenhouses, and the roof of the cow byre is visible beyond. (Grace Gore)

In 1944 Sir Cecil De Salis retired as chairman of the governors, and the now frail old gentleman received an illuminated address. He gave the school £1,000 to establish the De Salis Scholarship, and here he is receiving another £1,000 from Rex Crutchfield, chairman of the Pupils' Fund, to establish the Fidelis Scholarship. Both of these funds still enable the school to give financial assistance to former pupils.

In the immediate post-war period Bishopshalt boys dominated the Middlesex Grammar School Sports, being winners for several years running (no pun intended!). This is the victorious 1947 team with their coach, Mr Eric Wise. Back row, left to right: John Shepherd, Alan Watson, Bernard Stocks, David Gilbert. Front row: Bob Smith, John Swaisland, Ron Fennell.

The front garden of Bishopshalt in the spring of 1948. The area was always left to grow wild, the grass was never cut, and so it became known as 'The Wilderness'. In more recent times that title has fallen into disuse, because the grass is now regularly mown. However a host of daffodils can still be seen there every spring.

In October 1949 the school received a gift of three substantial oak chairs, adorned with the school coat-of-arms, for use by senior staff at morning assembly. The donors were the Randall family of Randall's Stores in Uxbridge. A.H. 'Bert' Randall was a pupil from 1910 to 1912, while his sons Alec (1935–9) and Norman (1939–44) followed later. The chairs are still in daily use. John Randall, MP for Uxbridge, is the son of Alec and the grandson of Bert. Behind the chairs we see the war memorial dedicated to the memory of the eighty-nine former pupils who gave their lives in the two world wars.

For years the Harvest Festival was a fixture in the school year, and here is the magnificent 1950 display. Encouraged by the 'Dig for Victory' campaign during the war, many parents were still growing fruit and vegetables in their own gardens. The produce was later distributed to needy residents in the district.

An art class in 1949, with the teacher Ronald Iden Coleman. Mr Coleman joined the staff in 1933 and retired in 1976, although during the war years he served in the RAF. He was a gifted watercolour artist, and the school is fortunate to possess about forty of his works on permanent display.

Lunch in the school hall in 1951. Sixth formers acted as 'heads of table', and after the saying of Grace the food was brought to them to distribute. Dinner money for the week was brought and collected on Monday mornings.

'Bring on the dancing girls!' The play being performed in the garden in July 1953 is *Tobias and the Angel*. The playwright James Bridie based the story on the apocryphal Book of Tobit.

In the mid-1950s work began on extending the school premises to the south, and one of the first buildings to be finished was the Assembly Hall, complete with a large stage and a gallery. This was a much-needed asset, and here we see the first concert in the hall in May 1956. Myfanwy Butler conducts the senior choir, with Mr E.A. Head at the detached console of the Walker pipe organ.

The hall enabled the school to mount a show every December, and in 1963 it was Shakespeare's *Much Ado About Nothing*. A humorous element was added by these enforcers of the law – the constable and 'the watch'. They are, from left to right, Keith Medler, John Weatherley, Geoffrey Willis, John Caldwell, Richard Bristow and Terry Barnett.

The year 1968 brought the retirement of Miss Muriel Kendall and Mr Harry Hawkins, who today would be described as deputy heads. The occasion led to a reunion of their former colleagues. Pictured here are, left to right, Mrs L. Smith, Miss K. Leonard, Miss M. Voigt, Miss Kendall, Mr Hawkins, Mr A.H. Holland, Mrs R. Hawkins, Mr E.T. Joy, Mrs M. Butler, Mr W.G. Moore, and Mr B. Butler.

The school's air-raid shelters, hastily installed in 1939, were still in position thirty years later, and for much of that period the 'cold war' brought fears that conflict might return. The photograph was taken just before the shelters were cleared in 1969, and the area became a much-needed car park. In the background is the recently completed caretaker's house, replacing the Victorian lodge.

The school appears in the lower half of this 1961 aerial photograph, with the extensions on the left now completed – a gymnasium, art and music rooms, workshops and classrooms. In the distance is still much open land. On the right is part of Hillingdon Cemetery, and beyond that is the former Lowe and Shawyer nursery which had closed in 1958 and was now awaiting redevelopment. On the left are the greenhouses of Milton Hutchings' nursery off Pield Heath Road.

By 1970 the Victorian conservatory was showing marked signs of deterioration, with damaged glass, rotting wood and some subsidence. The first conservatory to have a cast-iron frame was the Crystal Palace designed by Joseph Paxton for the Great Exhibition of 1851. The Bishopshalt conservatory was erected just seven years after that, and must be one of the earliest of its kind still standing. Headmaster Leslie Bather campaigned vigorously to get the building restored. After much fund-raising and persuasion the work was done, and here is the finished structure in November 1978. The Victorian wing of the school has since been designated a Grade II listed building. *(Brian Richardson)*

Among the fund-raising events for the conservatory appeal was a Victorian Garden Party held in July 1974, when visitors were encouraged to dress in the costume of the period. Here croquet is being played in the garden, much as the original owners of Bishopshalt would have done.

Many people helped in the restoration campaign, among them Sir John Betjeman, who sent a letter of support. Help also came from former pupil Sir Bernard Miles the actor, seen here with Dr Bather walking past the conservatory which was then partially wrapped in plastic sheets. Sir Bernard (later Lord Miles of Blackfriars) had brought the London Theatres cricket team to play a charity match against the school. He was accompanied by Millicent Martin and Leonard Rossiter.

Before the Civic Centre in Uxbridge was completed the Borough Council held their meetings in the school assembly hall. Here in July 1977 we see the mayor, Alderman A.H. Beasley, flanked by the deputy mayor and the chief executive. Unfortunately the dignity of the occasion was somewhat wrecked by the back-cloth of the latest school stage production – the Madpet Show, based on a popular TV series. *(Terry Beasley)*

At one time snowfall, and therefore snowballing, could be expected every winter, and it was traditional that the competition would be Sixth Form versus The Rest. Climate change means that this custom has probably been forgotten, for since January 1984 when this picture was taken there has not been a substantial fall of snow.

Above: The attractive setting of the school
has enticed film-makers on several
occasions. In 1980 scenes from a TV series
called *Forever Green*, starring John Alderton
and Pauline Collins, were shot here. The
mansion became a posh girls' school, and
here are some Bishopshalt girls as extras.
Back row, left to right: Amanda Joosten,
Elaine Wilson, Nicola Wareing, Samantha
Lever, Andra Moulson, Sarah Snelling.
Centre: Louise Dean, Babita Ghudial, Lisa
Silver, Alison Ferridge. Front row: Susan
McGuigan, Victoria Pearson, Ruth Wakling,
Emma Crook.

In October 1990 Hugh Laurie and Stephen
Fry came to film parts of an episode of the
TV series *Jeeves and Wooster*, and again
Bishopshalt became a posh girls' school. In
this picture Hugh Laurie, as Bertie Wooster,
is about to climb a holm oak in the school
garden at night.

In 1977 the school accepted its first non-selected entry, and so the change to comprehensive education began. By the late 1980s proposed reorganisation in the Borough meant that the school might lose its sixth form. This was not welcome. Application was then made for the new grant-maintained status, which was successful, and the degree of independence proved a great boon. Here, symbolically, we see the gates of opportunity being opened in September 1990. Barry Mordue and Matthew Briggs pull open the school gates for Claire Wilshire and Alison Hunt. (*Gazette*)

Grant-maintained status was eventually axed by the government, but in 1998 the school was designated an Arts College, specialising in music and the performing arts. The music block has been enlarged, and a dance/drama studio built. In 1992 the stage show was *The Sound Of Music*, with Claire Richards in the leading role as Maria. Claire later found fame as a member of the pop group Steps. The von Trapp children were, from left to right, Jamie McDermott, James Taylor, Natalie Howard, Daniela Carrasco, Laura Shave, Sarah Chamberlain and Jacqui Kirkpatrick. (*Gazette*)

Four headmasters. Clockwise from top left: John Miles (1929–49), John Wolfe (1950–70), David Bocock (from 2004) and Leslie Bather (1970–96). *(School/Author's Collection)*

10

Round & About

It is hard to believe that this tranquil spot is now a major road junction, where Corwell Lane and West Drayton Road cross Harlington Road. Today traffic proceeds incessantly from here to Heathrow Airport. This was always known as Merrimans Corner in the days when roadworks meant a man with a wheelbarrow.

Here in Colham Green about a hundred years ago road-menders pause to face the camera. With unsurfaced roads it was necessary from time to time for pot-holes and puddles to be filled in and levelled.

Hay-making time for the Shepherd family at Hubbards Farm, Colham Green in the 1920s. Frederick Shepherd stands behind his children John, Elsie and George. Frederick's wife's cousin Brenda is seated on the horse-drawn rake. John Shepherd (1917–2003) became a life-long and faithful servant of St John's church, and in 2006 a stained-glass window was dedicated there in his memory.

The two pictures on this page demonstrate the changing scene in the 1920s, as house-building developed apace on former farmland. From Vine Lane we look eastward along Blossom Way towards Sweetcroft Lane.

A view along the lower section of Sweetcroft Lane from the foot of Honey Hill. This scene was about to be changed by an extension of Hercies Road cutting through the field on the right.

Hillingdon Hospital from the air, *c.* 1930. Royal Lane is on the left, and Copperfield Avenue on the right. At this time the hospital lay completely to the north of Pield Heath Road, which is entirely hidden at the lower part of the picture by a continuous line of large trees. At this period the hospital was being transformed from a workhouse, which had been founded in 1747. *(B. Vogt)*

The front of the main workhouse building, which had been erected in about 1840. Originally this workhouse served the parish of Hillingdon only, but a change in the law in 1834 led to an enlarged building serving nine local parishes. In 1930 the Middlesex County Council assumed control, and the buildings began to develop as Hillingdon County Hospital. *(B. Vogt)*

A glimpse of two of the nursing staff at the hospital in the early 1930s. Sally Aslett, in the foreground, is keeping records, while a companion uses a treadle sewing machine to do some repairs. *(B. Vogt)*

To the west of the village lay the immense cut-flower nursery of Lowe and Shawyer, founded by Joseph Lowe in Kingston Lane in 1865. After 1897, when George Shawyer became a partner, the nursery expanded rapidly, specialising initially in chrysanthemums and roses for the London markets. Our photograph shows workers in a chrysanthemum house in about 1912.

From the 1920s many spring flowers were grown as well, and here we see a greenhouse full of Wedgewood iris in March 1927. The nursery, which eventually covered 199 acres, closed in 1958, and most of the site became Brunel University.

ACKNOWLEDGEMENTS

I n preparing this book I found helpful information in Daniel Lysons' historical account of Middlesex parishes (1800), in Rachel De Salis' *Hillingdon Through Eleven Centuries* (1926) and in Prebendary F.C. Tyler's booklet about St John's church.

I am sincerely grateful for the assistance given me by Angela Ball, Celia Callard, Patrick Dengel, Graham and Linda Dossett, the *Gazette* newspaper, Brenda Mothersole, Mary Ryan, the late John Shepherd, Philip Sherwood, Brian Shorthouse, P. Speechley, Betty Vogt, Audrey Wormald and Josephine Williams. The Local Studies staff at Uxbridge Central Library have been ever helpful, and I have been fortunate in having access to the extensive archives at Bishopshalt School.

Finally I thank my daughter Gill Clark, who prepared the text for publication.

All the photographs in this book are from the author's collection, unless otherwise credited at the end of the caption. The exception to this is the chapter on Bishopshalt School where, unless otherwise stated, the illustrations are from the school archive.

The Red Lion in 1967.